LONG AGO

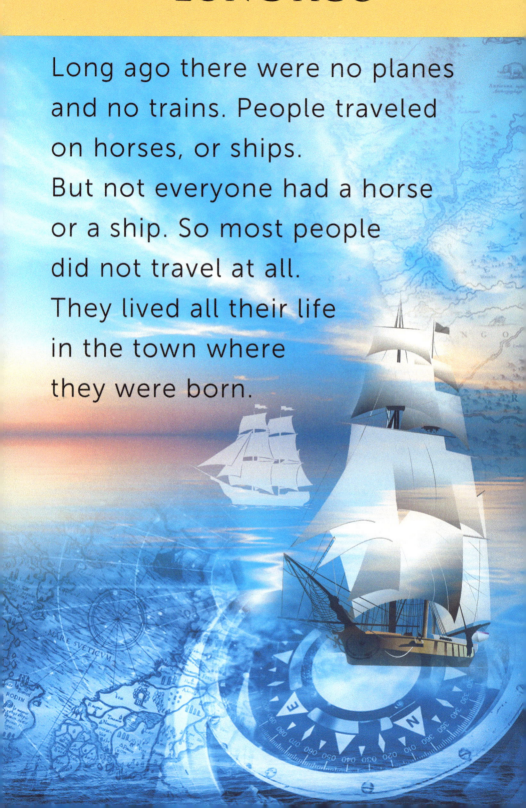

Long ago there were no planes
and no trains. People traveled
on horses, or ships.
But not everyone had a horse
or a ship. So most people
did not travel at all.
They lived all their life
in the town where
they were born.

It was boring!
People wanted to know about
far-away lands!
But there weren't
many books.
There were
no movies.
There was no TV,
no Internet.

Some sailors traveled to far-away lands. They told stories about strange animals.

People listened to their stories.

Then they told the stories to their friends.

And maybe they added a little bit to those stories.

Just to make them more exciting...

LEGENDS

For example, a sailor said:
"In Africa I saw a horse with
black and white stripes."
You and I know that he saw a zebra.
But in those days,
people didn't know about zebras.
There were no zoos!

So people heard this story, and told their friends: "In Africa there is a horse with blue and yellow stripes and red wings!" And everybody said: "Wow!"

Then their friends told this story
to other friends like this:
"In Africa there are animals that are
half-horse and half-snake.
They have four horns
on their head,
and red wings!"
And
everybody
said:
"Wow!"

But this was no longer a story
about a zebra.
It was a made-up story.
There are lots of stories
about things that don't exist
in real life.
We call them LEGENDS.
Let us meet some beasts
and monsters from old legends.

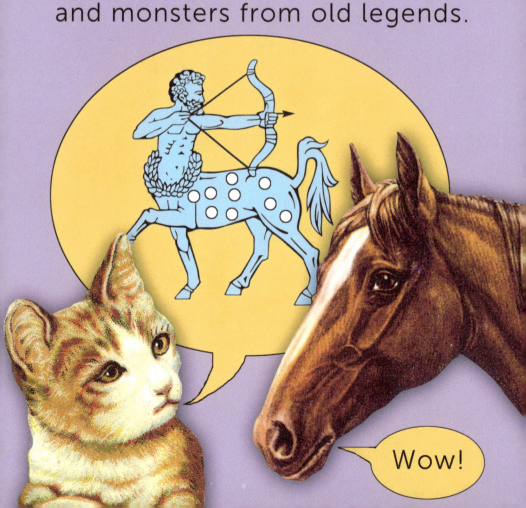

Wow!

THE GRIFFIN

Here is the griffin.
A griffin is half-lion and half-eagle.
Long ago people believed
griffins were real!

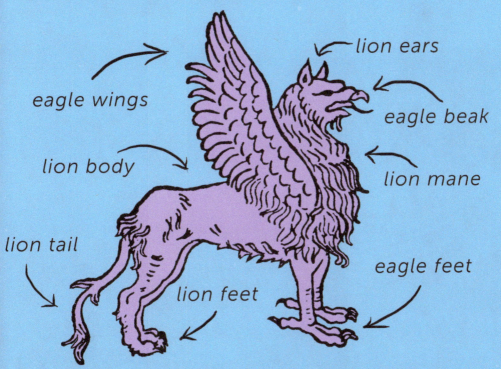

eagle wings

lion ears

eagle beak

lion body

lion mane

lion tail

eagle feet

lion feet

Pictures of Griffins on old seals.

THE GRIFFIN

What did griffins eat?
Legends say a griffin can steal
a pig or a sheep from a farm,
to feed its griffin-baby!

THE BASILISK

This is a basilisk.
It is half-rooster and half-dragon.
Everybody was afraid of basilisks.
Can you believe it?
I think it looks funny,
not scary at all!

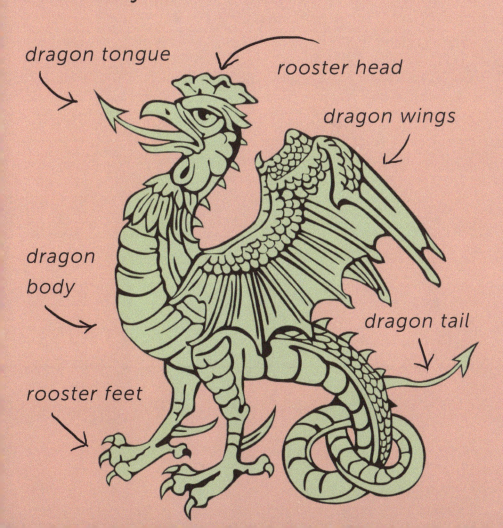

dragon tongue

rooster head

dragon wings

dragon body

dragon tail

rooster feet

SCARY OR FUNNY?

Some old legends tell us about half-people half-animals.

Do you think they are scary or just funny?

THE SPHYNX

The Sphynx was a legendary animal who had the head of a human and the body of a lion. Some sphynxes also had the wings of an eagle.

IN THE SEA

Long ago people did not know
about animals who live
in the ocean.
They thought these were
the same animals who live on land.
Only with fins.

They thought
a sea-horse
looked like this.

And a sea lion
looked
like
that!

SURPRISE!

Here is a real sea-horse.

And here is a real sea lion!

CROCODILES!

The legends about
scaly sea monsters
are not far from reality!
The salt-water crocodile is huge.
It kills more people
than any other animal in the world.
It even attacks sharks in the ocean!

Help!

When a crocodile sleeps,
only one half of its brain is asleep.
The other half is awake.
One eye is closed. The other is open
and looking for prey!

SEA SERPENTS

Old-time sailors also feared
a giant sea serpent, or sea snake.
They said it could sink a ship!

THE SEA SNAKE

Guess what:
The sea snake is a real animal.
It's not giant. It's small.
But it's the most dangerous snake
in the world.
One drop of its venom
can kill three people!
The good news is, it will never
attack you underwater.
But if you see it
on the beach RUN!

RUN!

Man,
I better
hide!

Photo: Christian Gloor

GIANT FISH

But why do old legends say
sea serpents are giant?
Maybe what sailors saw
was a giant oar-fish.
Here is an oar-fish found
on the beach in California.
Look how long it is!
Luckily for us, oar-fish
eat shrimp and jelly-fish.
They stay deep
in the ocean,
and run away from ships!

GIANT OCTOPUS

Sailors also feared a giant octopus!

Don't worry, no giant octopus exists in real life!!! If it were real, I would not go to the beach!

THE GIANT SQUID

Well, maybe
the giant octopus isn't real,
but the giant squid is!
It can grow as big
as a school bus!
Old legends
called it
the KRAKEN.

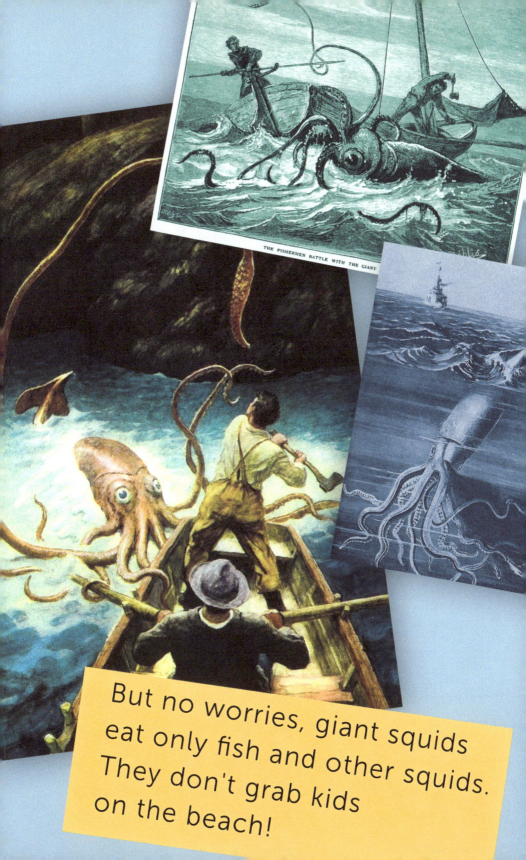

THE FISHERMEN BATTLE WITH THE GIANT

But no worries, giant squids eat only fish and other squids. They don't grab kids on the beach!

THE LION FISH

This is a fish monster
from old legends.

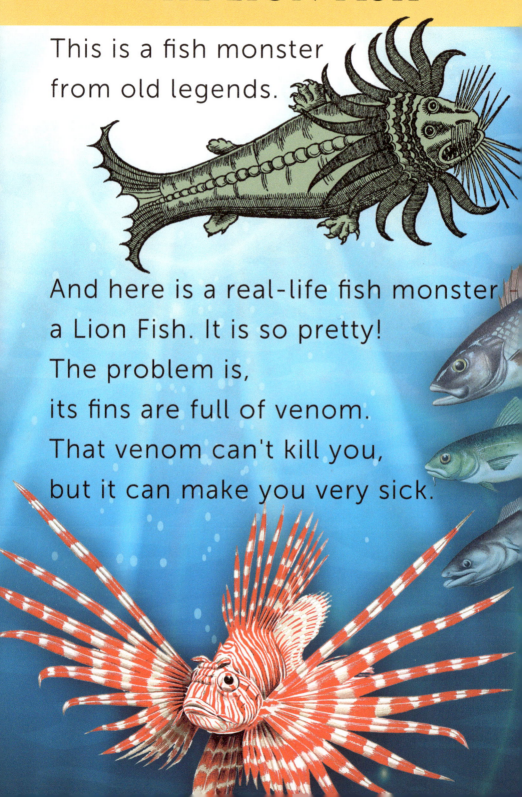

And here is a real-life fish monster—
a Lion Fish. It is so pretty!
The problem is,
its fins are full of venom.
That venom can't kill you,
but it can make you very sick.

THE BARRACUDA

We are not done with fish monsters!
There are more... the Barracuda!
If you stand a barracuda on its tail,
it's as tall as a tall person.
It attacks anything shiny,
because fish scales are shiny.
Don't wear jewelry in the water!
Barracudas even jump into boats
to attack people!

Uh-Oh!

THE CONE SNAIL

Another venomous
under-water monster
is the cone snail.
It's a sea snail. It lives in the ocean.
Look at these shells.

If you see them on the beach,
don't touch them!
If the snail is in the shell,
it can sting you.
Its poison is deadly.

As you can see, small monsters can be more dangerous than big ones. I would rather run into a giant squid than a cone snail!

Also, real-life monsters
can be more scary
than monsters from old legends!
I would rather run into this one

or this one,
than into
a real sea snake!
And you?

Sea snake?
Delicious!

Printed in the USA
CPSIA information can be obtained
at www.ICGtesting.com
LVHW062330030324
773452LV00016B/55